Diego Rivera

A Buddy Book
by
Sarah Tieck

ABDO
Publishing Company

VISIT US AT
www.abdopublishing.com

Published by ABDO Publishing Company, 4940 Viking Drive, Suite 622, Edina, Minnesota
55435. Copyright © 2007 by Abdo Consulting Group, Inc. International copyrights reserved
in all countries. No part of this book may be reproduced in any form without written
permission from the publisher.

Printed in the United States.

Contributing Editor: Michael P. Goecke
Graphic Design: Jane Halbert
Cover Photograph: Library of Congress
Interior Photographs: Clipart.com, Library of Congress, Juan Pablo López Manjarrez

Library of Congress Cataloging-in-Publication Data

Tieck, Sarah, 1976–
    Diego Rivera / Sarah Tieck.
        p. cm. — (First biographies. Set V)
    Includes index.
    ISBN 10 1-59679-785-1
    ISBN 13 978-1-59679-785-7
    1. Rivera, Diego, 1886-1957—Juvenile literature. 2. Painters—Mexico—Biography—
Juvenile literature. I. Rivera, Diego, 1886-1957. II.Title III. Series: Gosda, Randy T, 1959- .
First biographies. Set V.

ND259.R5T54 2006
759.972—dc22
                                                            2005031780

Table Of Contents

Who Is Diego Rivera? 4

Diego's Family 6

Growing Up 8

Discovering Art 11

Creating Murals 14

A Great Love 18

Politics And Art 21

A Long Career 26

Important Dates 30

Important Words 31

Web Sites 31

Index 32

Who Is Diego Rivera?

Diego Rivera

Diego Rivera was a famous Mexican artist. His paintings and murals were known for being big. He used many bright colors. Also, Diego's paintings showed his ideas about politics. They told stories about Mexico and its people.

Because of Diego, people learned about Mexico's culture. Diego helped other Mexican artists to be able to share their art.

Diego made many murals in the *Palacio Nacional* that showed the history of Mexico.

Diego's Family

Diego Rivera was born in Guanajuato, Mexico, on December 8, 1886.

Diego's mother was María del Pilar Barrientos. Diego's father was Diego Rivera Acosta. Diego had a twin brother named Carlos who died when he was about one year old. Diego also had a sister named María.

An outside view of the *Palacio Nacional* in Mexico City.

In 1893, Diego's family moved to Mexico City. Diego's mother took care of Diego and his sister. His father worked for the government.

Growing Up

There are many stories about Diego as a child. He grew up in a house full of ideas. Diego's father wanted to make life better for poor workers. He talked about his political ideas at home. This helped get Diego interested in politics.

Diego's murals often showed people working.

Diego loved to read his father's books. He also liked to go to school. Diego went to school at the San Carlos Academy of Fine Arts. This was a school for artists.

Diego always loved art. He started drawing when he was very little. He also liked to paint.

Some of the artwork that once hung in the San Carlos Academy of Fine Arts can be seen at the *Museo de San Carlos* today.

Diego finished school in 1906. He showed 26 paintings in a show for students. The governor saw Diego's paintings. He said Diego's paintings were good. He helped Diego get a scholarship to go to Europe. Diego could learn more about art there.

Discovering Art

Diego traveled all over the world so he could learn more about different styles of art. Diego spent time in France, Spain, and Italy.

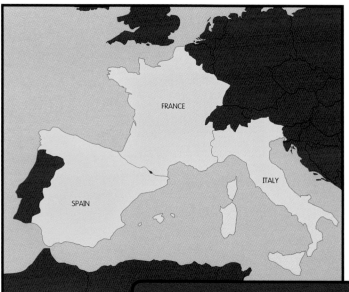

FRANCE

ITALY

SPAIN

Diego spent time in parts of Europe so he could learn about art. He visited countries such as Spain, France, and Italy.

Diego went to Spain first. Then in 1909, he moved to Paris, France. He learned from famous artists like Paul Cézanne. They taught him different ways to paint. Around 1917, Diego started to study a type of painting called Cubism. He painted in this style for several years.

These paintings are done in the Cubist style.

Creating Murals

In 1920, Diego went to Italy. There, he learned about fresco painting. Fresco painting is a very old way of painting. It is very hard. Artists paint on wet plaster. They have to go fast, so the plaster doesn't dry. Diego loved painting fresco murals. He was very good at it.

Diego at work on a fresco.

Diego's frescoes were unique. Few artists painted this way. Because his murals were on walls, many people could see them. More people started to notice his work. Also, other artists started to paint murals like Diego.

In 1931, people all around the world saw Diego's art. His paintings were shown at the Museum of Modern Art in New York City. Diego liked to paint pictures of the history and people of Mexico. People liked the bright colors and the stories Diego's paintings told.

A mural from *Palacio de Bellas Artes* in Mexico City. Diego used many bright colors.

After that, Diego was asked to paint many murals. In July 1932, Diego started painting one of his most famous murals. It was in the United States at the Detroit Institute of Arts. Diego painted an auto plant and its workers. The painting was finished in March 1933.

A Great Love

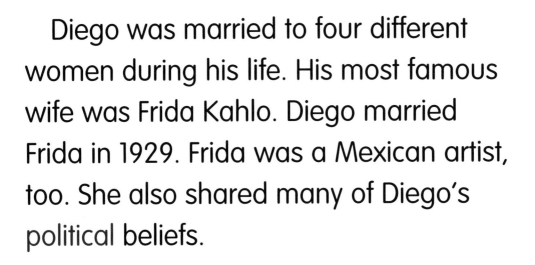

Diego was married to four different women during his life. His most famous wife was Frida Kahlo. Diego married Frida in 1929. Frida was a Mexican artist, too. She also shared many of Diego's political beliefs.

Diego often painted himself and Frida in his murals.

Frida Kahlo

Diego and Frida's home and studio was in Mexico City.

Politics And Art

Diego and Frida were Communists. Many people didn't like their political ideas. These people thought Communism was harmful. Diego and Frida didn't care. They believed in Communism.

In 1937, Diego and Frida helped a man named Leon Trotsky. Trotsky was a leader of the Communist party. He wasn't allowed in his own country because of his political beliefs. Many people didn't like that Frida and Diego helped Trotsky come to Mexico to live.

Leon Trotsky (center) is pictured in Diego's mural at the *Palacio de Bellas Artes*.

Diego also liked to show his political beliefs in his paintings and murals.

Diego showed history and his political beliefs in many frescoes.

He did this in a fresco at Rockefeller Center in New York City. Diego painted a scene of workers in Moscow, Russia. He also painted a Communist leader named Vladimir Lenin.

People didn't like what Diego painted. They wanted him to change his mural. Diego wouldn't change his painting. The Rockefellers told him to stop painting and leave.

Diego returned to Mexico. In February 1934, workers with axes destroyed Diego's fresco painting. People didn't agree with his political beliefs. He was sad and angry.

After Diego's Rockefeller Center mural was destroyed, he painted another one in Mexico City (above). It is at *Palacio de Bellas Artes*. Lenin is included in the mural (right).

A Long Career

For many years, Diego and Frida traveled the world and worked on their art. In 1947, Diego painted a mural of Mexico's history. Some people say this is his best painting. It was called *Dream of a Sunday Afternoon in Alameda Park.*

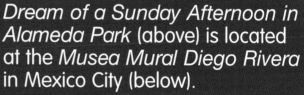

Dream of a Sunday Afternoon in Alameda Park (above) is located at the *Musea Mural Diego Rivera* in Mexico City (below).

Frida Kahlo with Diego Rivera.

In 1954, Frida died. She had been sick for many years. Diego was very sad to lose Frida.

In 1955, Diego found out that he was sick. On November 24, 1957, Diego died in Mexico City. Today, people can still see many of Diego's murals and paintings. He is remembered as a great painter.

Some of Diego's work is at *Palacio de Bellas Artes* in Mexico City.

Important Dates

December 8, 1886 Diego Rivera and his twin brother Carlos are born.

1906 Diego graduates from the San Carlos Academy of Fine Arts.

1909 Diego begins to study art in France.

1913 Diego begins to paint in the Cubist style.

1914 Diego's first solo art show for the Societé des Artistes Indépendants.

1920 Diego travels to Italy. He learns about fresco painting there. This is the style of painting he'll become known for.

1929 Diego marries Frida Kahlo.

1931 Diego's work is shown at the Museum of Modern Art in New York City.

1934 Diego's mural at Rockefeller Center is destroyed. People don't like that his political beliefs are shown in the painting.

1937 Diego and Frida help Communist Leon Trotsky come to Mexico.

1940 Diego and Frida divorce. Diego marries Frida again.

1947 Diego paints *Dream of a Sunday Afternoon in Alameda Park*. Some say this mural is his best.

1954 Frida dies.

November 24, 1957 Diego dies.

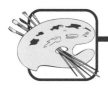

Important Words

Communism social and economic system in which everything is owned by the government and given to the people as needed. People who believe in Communism are called Communists.

Cubism a type of art that was popular in the early 1900s. Cubism shows an object from many different viewpoints at the same time.

culture the ideas, arts, and way of life of a group of people.

fresco a painting technique where artists paint on wet plaster.

mural a large picture, usually on a wall.

plaster a thick, sticky mixture of lime, sand, and water that is used to cover walls. It becomes hard when it dries.

political having to do with government.

unique something that is special or different.

Web Sites

To learn more about Diego Rivera, visit ABDO Publishing Company on the World Wide Web. Web site links about Diego Rivera are featured on our Book Links page. These links are routinely monitored and updated to provide the most current information available.

www.abdopublishing.com

Index

Acosta, Diego Rivera **6, 7, 8, 9**

Barrientos, María del Pilar **6, 7**

Cézanne, Paul **12**

Communism . . .**21, 22, 24, 30**

Cubism **12, 13, 30**

Detroit Institute of Arts **17**

Europe **10**

France **11, 12, 30**

fresco **14, 15, 23, 24, 25, 30**

Guanajuato, Mexico **6**

Italy **11, 14, 30**

Kahlo, Frida **18, 19, 20, 21, 22, 26, 28, 30**

Lenin, Vladimir **24, 25**

Mexico **4, 5, 6, 7, 16, 18, 22, 25, 26, 30**

Mexico City **7, 16, 20, 25, 27, 29**

Musea Mural Diego Rivera **27**

Museum of Modern Art **16, 30**

New York City **16, 24, 30**

Palacio de Bellas Artes **16, 22, 25, 29**

Palacio Nacional **5, 7**

Paris, France **12**

Rivera, Carlos **6, 30**

Rivera, María **6**

Rockefeller Center **24, 25, 30**

San Carlos Academy of Fine Arts **9, 10, 30**

Societé des Artistes Indépendants **30**

Spain **11, 12**

Trotsky, Leon **22, 30**

United States **17**